All Things— Even Frisky

by **Matilda Nordtvedt**

A Beka Book.
A MINISTRY OF
PENSACOLA CHRISTIAN COLLEGE
PENSACOLA, FLORIDA 32523-9160

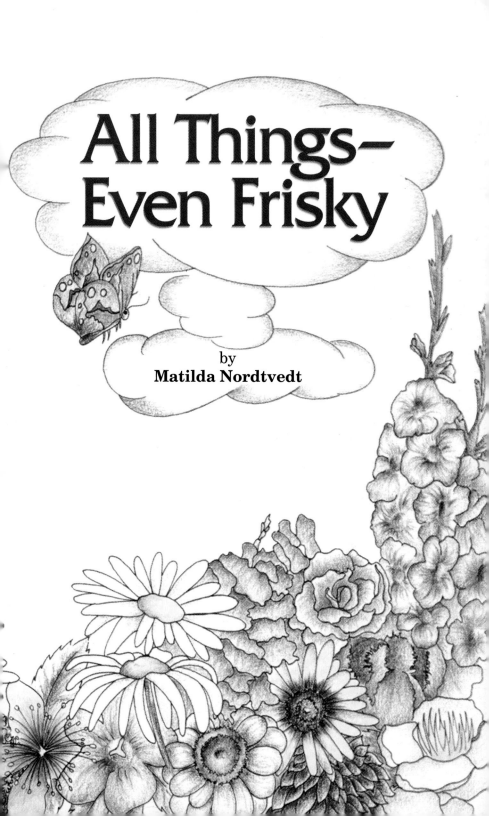

All Things—
Even Frisky

by
Matilda Nordtvedt

A Beka Book® ◢◢ Reading Program

Handbook for Reading *(grades 1–3)*
Primary Bible Reader *(grades 1–3)*
Read & Think Skill Sheets *(grades 3–6)*

1st

Fun with Pets
Tiptoes
Stepping Stones
Secrets and Surprises
The Bridge Book
Animals in the
    Great Outdoors
Kind and Brave
Aesop's Fables
Strong and True
Down by the Sea

2nd

Story Tree
Treasure Chest
Hidden Treasure
No Longer a Nobody *(novel)*
Paths of Gold
Sunshine Meadows
Silver Sails
All Things—Even Frisky *(novel)*
Growing Up Where
    Jesus Lived
All Kinds of Animals

3rd

Paths to Adventure
Footprints
Crossroads
Pilgrim Boy *(novel)*
Secret in the Maple Tree *(novel)*
Better Bridges
Worlds of Wonder
Pilgrim's Progress

4th

Song of the Brook *(novel)*
Saved at Sea *(novel)*
Salute to Courage
Liberty Tree
Flags Unfurled
Trails to Explore
Adventures in Other Lands
    (Speed/Comprehension)

5th

Rosa *(novel)*
Noah Webster: A Man Who
    Loved Words
Beyond the Horizon
Windows to the World
Of America 1
Adventures in Nature
    (Speed/Comprehension)

6th

Billy Sunday
Message of the Mountain *(novel)*
Mountain Pathways
Voyage of Discovery
Of America II
Adventures in Greatness
    (Speed/Comprehension)

Table of Contents

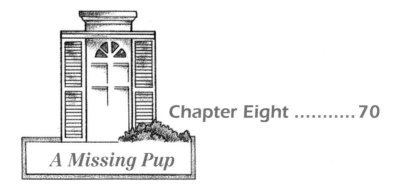

Table of Contents Continued

MISSING!

1

Frisky meets Aunt Kate

Billy was worried. He looked anxiously at the tiny black-and-white puppy sleeping in his arms. What if Aunt Kate didn't like Frisky? What if she wouldn't let Billy keep him?

Billy brushed a lock of sandy-colored hair out of his round blue eyes and stared at the rosy sky behind the housetops in the distance. But he didn't notice the beautiful colors of the sunset. He was thinking about the thin, jumpy woman who had visited them two Christmases ago. She was Mother's younger sister, but she seemed older.

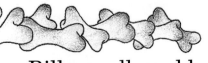

Billy swallowed hard as he sat down on the back steps with Frisky in his arms. Why did Dad have to bring somebody like Aunt Kate to live with them, anyway?

"I have a new job, Billy," Dad had explained, "which will keep me traveling and away from home much of the time. Mrs. Stevens has been a good helper since Mother died, but she can't stay nights, so I had to get someone else. Aunt Kate is your mother's sister, you know. We must be kind to her."

Billy sighed as he ran his hand back and forth over Frisky's smooth back. "Please, God," he prayed, "make Aunt Kate like Frisky. I don't care so much if she likes me or not,

but please make her like Frisky."
Billy brushed away a couple of tears
that trickled down his freckled, up-
turned nose and buried his face in
Frisky's soft fur.

The sound of a car in the drive-
way made him look up quickly. Dad
and Aunt Kate! Slowly he stood up,
letting Frisky tumble down the
steps. He watched silently as Dad
came around the car and opened the
door for Aunt Kate.

Just as thin as ever, he thought as
his aunt stepped out of the car. Everything about Aunt Kate was thin
from her small nose to her pointed
chin. Her dark hair pulled back
tightly from her face made her look
older than she really was, and her

large, hazel eyes seemed too big for the rest of her face.

Dad, who seemed even bigger than usual beside Aunt Kate, was twitching his nose and twirling the end of his reddish mustache—as he always did when he wasn't sure how things would turn out.

Billy started slowly toward them.

"Billy, dear!" exclaimed Aunt Kate, stooping over and giving him a kiss on the cheek. She started to say more, but her words turned to a little shriek. Frisky was jumping around her legs, yipping delightedly.

"Oh! Oh! A horrid dog!" she cried. "He's biting me! He's ruining my stockings! Get him away from me! Quick! Shoo!"

4

"He's just a pup, Aunt Kate," said Billy, making a dive for Frisky. His heart made a dive, too. It was just as he had feared. Aunt Kate didn't like Frisky.

Billy knew he should help carry in Aunt Kate's things, but if he put Frisky down he might yip at her heels again. He waited until his aunt was safely inside, then released the wriggling puppy. Picking up the suitcase that was left, he walked into the house.

Billy had no sooner set the suitcase down on the kitchen floor when he heard another shriek. "Oh, that horrid dog! Take him out of here!"

Billy, with a sinking heart, swooped his pet up into his arms

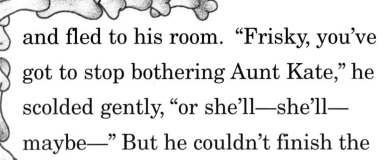

and fled to his room. "Frisky, you've got to stop bothering Aunt Kate," he scolded gently, "or she'll—she'll—maybe—" But he couldn't finish the sentence.

Dad was showing Aunt Kate to her room down the hall. Billy could hear her voice clearly.

"Really, George, dogs in the house are a terrible nuisance. They make me nervous. If Billy must have a dog, he should certainly keep him out in the garage!"

Billy didn't wait to hear more. Clutching Frisky tightly in his arms, he ran out of the house, across the yard, and—forgetting to knock—burst into Uncle John's cozy little kitchen.

Uncle John was everybody's uncle, even though he had no living relatives in Burlingham. He was the town's handyman who repaired clocks, sharpened ice skates, painted signs, and raised strawberries. Uncle John was getting bald, had small, merry eyes and a big nose, and walked with a limp. He was washing his supper dishes when Billy burst into the kitchen.

"Hi, Billy," he said, rubbing his wet hands on his pants. "Nice to have a visit from you and Frisky. Sit down." He offered Billy a chair. "How about a couple of doughnuts left over from supper?"

Billy shook his head as he sank into the chair, still clutching Frisky tightly.

7

Uncle John raised his eyebrows. "No doughnuts? Something must be wrong, Billy."

Billy swallowed hard, but the lump in his throat wouldn't go away. He bit his lip and brushed angrily at his eyes, but the tears came anyway.

"It's—it's Aunt Kate. She doesn't like Frisky. I know she'll never let him sleep with me. She said I should keep him in the garage." Billy buried his wet face in Frisky's soft, white fur to hide his tears.

Uncle John paced back and forth in the little kitchen with his hands clasped behind him as he always did when he was thinking. Suddenly he stopped. Billy lifted his tear-stained

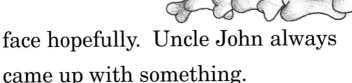

face hopefully. Uncle John always came up with something.

"She wants to keep him in the garage, eh?"

Billy nodded. "If he's out there he'll cry all night, Uncle John, and then the neighbors won't be able to sleep, and I'll have to get rid of him for sure. You remember how he cried those first nights I had him until I took him in bed with me."

Uncle John nodded. "Yes, he still misses his mother. I have a plan, Billy, that I think will work. But first, you must be willing to compromise."

"Compro—what?" asked Billy, puzzled.

"That's a big word that means two people settling something by both giving in a little. You want Frisky in your room and Aunt Kate wants him out in the garage. Why don't you compromise by fixing him a bed in the basement. Your aunt would probably agree to that."

"But what if he gets cold and cries all night?" worried Billy.

Uncle John went to a cupboard and pulled out a hot water bottle. "You fill this with hot water, wrap it in a piece of cloth, and put it in Frisky's bed. He'll be so warm and cozy he'll think he's in bed with you!"

Uncle John hobbled into the next room and came back with a clock.

"Wrap this up and put it in his box, too. The ticking will remind him of his mother's heartbeat and make him feel content. And now, before you go, let's bring our problem to the Lord."

Billy bowed his head while Uncle John prayed about Frisky and Aunt Kate. Was God really that interested in a ten-year-old boy and his pup? It sounded like it, by the way Uncle John was praying.

After the prayer Billy felt so much better that he decided to have one of Uncle John's doughnuts after all. Armed with the hot water bottle and clock, he picked up Frisky, said goodbye to his friend, and ran home.

11

2
A Bed for Frisky

Aunt Kate gave in to the basement idea but didn't seem too happy about it. Carefully Billy fixed up a cozy little bed for his pup. At first Frisky didn't want to stay in it, but after Billy petted him a while he curled up next to the hot water bottle and fell fast asleep. Billy heaved a sigh of relief. Now if he would only stay asleep and not bother Aunt Kate.

Billy skipped his bedtime snack. Somehow he didn't feel at home in the kitchen with Aunt Kate sitting there knitting. He was all settled in

bed when Aunt Kate came in. She sat down on a chair beside the bed.

"I think your dog will be much happier in the basement, Billy," she said. "It's so much better to have him there than in your room. You understand, don't you?"

Billy didn't really, but he nodded anyway. Aunt Kate kissed him on the cheek, turned out the light, and closed the door.

Billy lay in the dark trying to sort out his feelings. Aunt Kate was mean because she didn't like Frisky. But she did agree to his sleeping in the basement instead of the garage, so maybe she wasn't *all* mean.

Dad was at a meeting tonight and would leave tomorrow for a long trip. Billy felt lonesome thinking about it. He'd been lonesome a lot since Mother had died. Getting the puppy had helped. But what if Aunt Kate made him get rid of Frisky? A big lump came into Billy's throat when he thought about it. Then he remembered Uncle John.

Uncle John had come to his rescue more than once. He remembered the day the crippled man had explained how Billy could become a member of God's family.

"All of us have done wrong, Billy," he had said, drawing a line at the bottom of a piece of paper. "We're way down here, and God is way up here, sinless and holy." He drew another line at the top of the page.

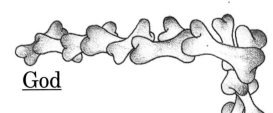

God

Man

"We can't reach God no matter how hard we try to be good. But God loved us so much He sent His Son to take the punishment for our sins on the cross."

Then Uncle John drew a cross joining the two lines.

God
✝
Man

"When we are sorry for our sins, believe that Jesus paid for them on the cross, and receive Him as our Savior, God forgives us and makes us His children. Have you ever received Him, Billy?"

"I don't know how," he had murmured.

"You just wait a minute," he had said as he hobbled into the other room. When he came back he was carrying a small, wrapped package.

"I have a present for you, Billy," he said, holding out the package.

"Thanks, Uncle John." Billy had grinned as he took it and eagerly unwrapped it. "A book! That's neat, Uncle John. Thanks a lot."

"It's the New Testament part of the Bible. I hope you'll read it."

"Sure I will," Billy had said. "I like to read."

"How did that book become yours, Billy?"

"I don't know. You gave it to me and I—I just took it."

"That's right," Uncle John had said, "and that's the way we receive Jesus as our Savior. We can't see Him, but we believe what the Bible says about Him and take Him by faith. If you simply invite Him into your life, Billy, He will come in and make you God's son. He will be with you always and someday take you to heaven."

Billy had bowed his head in Uncle John's kitchen that day and asked Jesus to forgive his sins, make his heart clean, and come into his life. He had felt happy and close to God after that.

Uncle John had come over and talked to Billy's mother, too, when she was sick. After he left, Mother had called Billy to her bedside. With a smile on her face, she had told him she was ready for heaven and some day would meet Billy there.

Just thinking about seeing Mother again made Billy feel better inside. Even if Dad was leaving and Aunt Kate didn't understand about pups, there were always Uncle John and Jesus—and someday Mother. So everything wasn't bad, decided Billy as he fell asleep.

Billy didn't know how long he had been sleeping when he heard the whining. He was too sleepy to pay attention at first, but suddenly he knew what it was. Frisky was crying in the basement and maybe waking Aunt Kate!

Billy jumped out of bed, slipped out of his room, and quietly made his way down the basement stairs. Frisky stood shivering at the bottom, yapping piteously.

"Frisky," whispered Billy, picking up the forlorn puppy, "why aren't you sleeping? Don't you know you'll wake up Aunt Kate and then we'll really be in trouble!" He carried the puppy back to his box in the corner and put him in. But Frisky jumped out. He wanted to play even if it was the middle of the night, and for once Billy didn't feel like playing.

He crouched sadly by the box while Frisky jumped around him.

"I know, the water bottle is cold!" he suddenly exclaimed to himself. "I'll fill it with hot water again, and maybe Frisky will go back to sleep." Sure enough, it worked. Frisky snuggled up contentedly in the box next to the warm bottle.

When he was sure Frisky was asleep, Billy quietly started up the basement steps. Then his heart almost stopped beating. Aunt Kate was standing at the top of the stairs.

Billy didn't look at Aunt Kate. He was sure she was angry for being disturbed in the middle of the night. Tears rushed to his eyes. He would have to explain and stick up for Frisky.

"He was cold," Billy managed to say, "but I filled the hot water bottle, so I don't think he'll cry anymore."

"And I imagine *you* are cold, too, young man!" she exclaimed. "Bare feet on that cement floor! You'll catch pneumonia. Get back into bed at once!"

Billy didn't need Aunt Kate's help to get into bed, but she followed him into his room and pulled the covers over him. Suddenly his aunt's face lost the angry frown.

"You worry about your pup, Billy, but I worry about *you*," she said softly, tucking the covers around his shoulders.

Billy looked at her in surprise. He hadn't noticed before how much

Aunt Kate's eyes were like Mother's. For an instant he imagined it was his own mother tucking him into bed.

3

Puddles and a Fall

Billy woke up without being called the next morning. He could hear sounds coming from the kitchen, so he knew Aunt Kate was up. He would have liked to sleep longer this second day of spring vacation, but he didn't care. He had to take care of Frisky.

Frisky stood waiting at the bottom of the basement stairs, wagging his tail and begging to be taken upstairs. Billy noticed a puddle behind him.

"Oh, oh, better wipe that up," he decided, looking for a rag.

Aunt Kate didn't say much at breakfast—didn't even mention being awakened by Frisky the night before. Billy felt relieved. A smile played around his lips as he dug his spoon into his oatmeal.

Aunt Kate stood up to bring the toast. Suddenly she stopped and looked accusingly at Frisky, playing happily with a rubber mouse. "You—you naughty little thing! Billy, look! A puddle!"

Sure enough, Frisky had made a mistake on the shiny kitchen floor.

"In the kitchen of all places!" gasped Aunt Kate. "Billy, get a mop and bucket. I'm going to wash this floor!"

Then Billy saw something Aunt Kate didn't see —another puddle right behind her. "Aunt Kate," he began in a hoarse whisper, "watch out!" But it was too late. Stepping back from the offending pup, Aunt Kate stepped in the second puddle. Before Billy's horrified eyes, her feet flew out from under her, and she landed in a heap on the floor.

Billy didn't know what to do first—get the mop or help his aunt to her feet. Aunt Kate left him no doubt. "Get that horrid dog out of this kitchen," she hissed between clenched teeth as she struggled to get up. Billy didn't need to be told twice.

"Frisky, indeed!" stormed Aunt Kate as she limped about mopping the kitchen floor with a great quantity of soap and water. "Nuisance, if you ask me! That's a much better name for him. I tell you, Billy, I just can't put up with this. I'm sorry, but I'm afraid you'll just have to get rid of that pup, or I'll have to leave. Can't you give him to a friend and visit him once in a while?"

Billy didn't answer. He couldn't, because of the lump in his throat. Silently he slipped down to the basement, picked up Frisky, and went outside. "Uncle John will help me," he said. "I'll go to see Uncle John."

Uncle John was busy painting a sign when Billy knocked at his back

door. He kept right on working while Billy told his sad tale. "And just because he puddles on the kitchen floor she says I have to get rid of him. Uncle John, why doesn't God make Aunt Kate like Frisky like I asked Him to?"

Uncle John stood back and looked at his work before he answered. "Well, Billy, you can't expect your aunt to be happy about puddles on the kitchen floor. As for God answering your prayer, did you ever think that He might be waiting for a little cooperation from you?"

"What do you mean?" puzzled Billy.

"Take a man without a job. Does he sit at home and pray that God will give him one?"

"N-no," admitted Billy. "I think he prays while he's looking for one."

"Exactly," answered Uncle John, wiping his paint brush. "It's up to you to do all you can to make Aunt Kate like Frisky. Why don't you get on your bike, go down to the library, and check out a book on training dogs? Frisky may stay here with me while you're gone."

Billy ran home to get his library card, then hopped on his bike and pedaled to the public library. He asked the lady behind the desk if she had any books on training dogs.

"Certainly," she answered with a smile and told him where to look on the shelves.

Choosing one of the books, Billy checked it out and started back to Uncle John's on his bike. He pedaled as fast as he could go with the book in his bike basket. He could hardly wait to find out what it said. He hadn't realized that he could train Frisky to behave in a way that even Aunt Kate would approve of. Good old Uncle John. He could count on him every time!

4

The Deserted House

Billy worked hard. He put Frisky outside every hour, took him for walks, and spread newspapers on part of the basement floor.

"He's learning, Uncle John," he reported joyously on Saturday. "He's an awfully smart pup. He hasn't had an accident since yesterday afternoon. And Aunt Kate hasn't gotten mad at him lately. She still calls him Nuisance, though," he added sadly.

Uncle John put his hand on Billy's shoulder. "Don't you worry, young man," he said. "Everything is going to turn out all right."

Uncle John's words made Billy feel a lot better.

Billy hurried home from school on Monday. *How had Aunt Kate made out with Frisky all day,* he wondered. Anxiously he opened the back door. Frisky came tumbling to meet him. After hugging his pup, Billy noticed his aunt sitting in a straight chair by the kitchen table, knitting. She didn't look happy. Billy's heart sank.

"Hi, Aunt Kate," he said without much enthusiasm.

"Hello," answered Aunt Kate, glancing up from her knitting. She didn't smile.

Why was she sad? Billy wondered, *Was it Frisky?* Billy hardly dared

ask, but he had to know. "How was—Frisky, Aunt Kate?" he ventured timidly.

"Nuisance!" corrected his aunt, pausing in her knitting only long enough to give the pup a withering glance.

"You mean—" faltered Billy.

"Yes, twice. I just don't know how many more days I'm going to be able to put up with him."

Billy sat forlornly on the back steps and chewed his apple. "Please, God," he prayed desperately, then stopped. He had prayed about Frisky and Aunt Kate so many times lately, but God didn't seem to pay any attention.

"Hey, Billy!"

Billy turned to see Pete Simmons hurrying around the corner of the house toward him. His curly black hair was more tousled than ever, and his brown eyes shone with excitement. He plopped down on the steps beside Billy.

Billy forgot about his problem with Frisky. That look in Pete's eye always meant adventure.

Pete didn't waste any time. "You know the deserted house out by Stony Creek?" He looked at Billy sideways.

Billy nodded. "Yeah, I know." Everybody in Burlingham knew about the Stony Creek deserted house.

Pete leaned over and picked a leaf off the lilac bush by the steps. "No-

body goes there because Old Man Hitchcock died alone in the house," he said as he tore the leaf into little pieces and dropped them on the step.

Billy nodded. "Yeah, I know."

Pete edged a little closer to Billy and lowered his voice. "Nobody goes there except Old Man Hitchcock's ghost!"

Billy looked over his shoulder uneasily as if Mr. Hitchcock's ghost were right there listening to their conversation and not approving of it. But he couldn't let Pete know how he felt. Pete was bigger and could run faster than he. Billy couldn't let him be braver, too.

"Aw, I don't believe in any old ghosts," he said, trying to sound careless.

Pete stood up and looked at him with a frown. "You don't believe in ghosts? Well, my dad said old Sid McClennan *saw* Mr. Hitchcock's ghost. When he went to the house to get doorknobs and stuff for his junk shop, he saw the ghost and even heard him talking to himself."

Billy's spine began to feel prickly. "What did he look like?" he demanded in a hoarse whisper, forgetting to sound careless.

Pete shook his head. "Sid was too scared to take a good look. He ran all the way home, and now he says

he wouldn't go back there for all the doorknobs in King County!"

Frisky was jumping around Billy's legs, yapping for attention. Billy picked him up and stroked him, but his mind wasn't on Frisky. He was thinking about Old Man Hitchcock's ghost roaming around in the Stony Creek deserted house.

Pete had a faraway look in his eyes. "I've always kind of wanted to see a ghost," he said.

Billy gulped. What was Pete thinking of?

Pete gave Billy a quick glance. "But I suppose you'd be scared to go have a look at him."

Billy *was* scared. Just talking about the ghost in the deserted

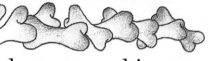

house gave him goose bumps, but he'd *never* admit that to Pete.

"Scared?" he answered scornfully. "Who's scared? You are."

Pete shook his head. "Not me. I'd go to the deserted house any time to see that old ghost."

Billy glanced at Pete out of the corner of his eye. He couldn't mean what he was saying. He was only fooling. Well, Billy could pretend, too. He shrugged carelessly. "You say when," he said.

Pete didn't answer right away. When he did, the shivers went up and down Billy's spine. "How about Saturday afternoon?" he said in a loud whisper.

"You mean th-this Saturday?"
The words stuck in Billy's throat.

Pete nodded. "Right after lunch.
Don't forget. I have to go now." And
Pete sauntered off.

Billy watched Pete go, then slowly
stood up, and walked into the house.
Somehow it seemed safer inside,
even if Aunt Kate was angry with
Frisky.

5

Good for Something

When Billy burst into the kitchen the next day after school, his heart almost stood still. Where was Frisky?

Aunt Kate was busy at the sink. She didn't turn around when Billy came in. Something was wrong.

"Hi, Aunt Kate," he said. "Where's—where's Frisky?"

Aunt Kate's back looked stiff.

"He's in the basement being punished," she answered crisply.

Billy heaved a sigh of relief. At least she hadn't given him away! "Punished?" he questioned.

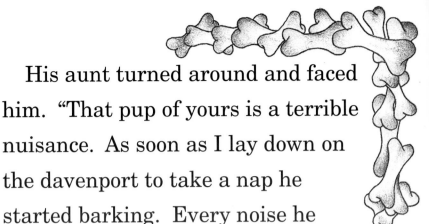

His aunt turned around and faced him. "That pup of yours is a terrible nuisance. As soon as I lay down on the davenport to take a nap he started barking. Every noise he heard he'd jump up and growl. I couldn't get a minute's rest."

"That's because he's taking care of you, Aunt Kate," interrupted Billy eagerly. "He's a watchdog and—"

"He is Nuisance, Puddles, and Rascal," snapped Aunt Kate, "and I could think of a lot of other suitable names for him. He's driving me frantic!"

Billy turned away to hide the tears that rushed to his eyes, but not before Aunt Kate noticed.

"Here," she said, "have a couple of cookies. They're oatmeal and should be good for you. And," she added grudgingly, "I suppose you can let the pup up now. I hope he's learned something by this time."

Billy ate the cookies on the back steps while Frisky frolicked around his feet, grateful for the small pieces Billy held out to him. Suddenly Billy knew he must talk to Uncle John. Wiping the crumbs off his mouth with the back of his hand, he ran across the yard to his friend's house. Frisky tagged along at his heels.

Uncle John listened patiently while Billy told him of Frisky's latest antics. "I know he was just trying to protect Aunt Kate, Uncle John," he said, "but she thinks he's a nuisance. I've prayed and prayed that God would make her like Frisky. Why doesn't God answer my prayer?"

The old man's eyes twinkled. "He will, Bill. He will. You just wait. God is never in a hurry, but He's never too late. Often He answers our prayers much differently from what we expect, but His ways are always best in the long run. There's a verse in the Bible about this I like very much— 'All things work together for good to them that love God.' That's Romans 8:28 if you want to look it up."

Billy thought about Uncle John's words as he undressed for bed that night. Dropping to his knees beside the bed, he prayed as usual, then added, "And please, Jesus, don't forget about Frisky and Aunt Kate. Uncle John said You are never too late." Then he jumped into bed and was soon fast asleep.

At first Billy heard the barking only in his dreams, then suddenly he was awake. He jumped out of bed and raced for the basement. He was afraid this would decide Frisky's fate for sure. The pup hadn't barked at night for a long time. What would Aunt Kate say?

Billy took the basement steps two at a time. He had to stop Frisky

before he woke up Aunt Kate with his
barking. But it was too late already.
He could hear her coming down the
hall.

"Frisky," pleaded Billy, as he
reached for the jumping pup, "stop
that barking!" But Frisky wouldn't
stop. Billy could hear Aunt Kate coming down the basement stairs. His
heart sank. Suddenly he saw what
was making Frisky bark. Aunt Kate
saw it at the same time.

"A mouse!" she shrieked.

Sure enough, Frisky had cornered
a small mouse and was jumping excitedly around the scared little creature.

Aunt Kate fled to the safety of the
first floor, shutting the door firmly
behind her.

Billy couldn't understand either
Aunt Kate or Frisky. What was so
bad about a little old mouse, anyway?

Suddenly the mouse darted past
Frisky and disappeared. Billy
grabbed his barking dog and ran up
to the kitchen. He found a white-
faced Aunt Kate pacing the floor.

"Oh, that horrid mouse!" she
cried. "I can't stand mice! What if
he comes into my bedroom while I'm
sleeping?" She shuddered and
looked helplessly at Billy.

Billy felt sorry for Aunt Kate.
Afraid of a tiny little mouse?

"I know where there's a trap,
Aunt Kate," he said. "If you'll give
me some cheese, I'll set the trap

down in the basement, and we'll catch the mouse."

Aunt Kate hastily found some cheese in the refrigerator and gave a piece to Billy. As Billy put Frisky down and started for the basement to set the mousetrap, he heard Aunt Kate say, "Imagine sleeping in the same house with a mouse! Frisky, I'm glad you discovered him. Guess you're good for something after all!"

Billy turned around and looked. He couldn't believe his eyes! Aunt Kate was actually petting Frisky and letting him lick her hand!

6

New Tricks

Pete caught up with Billy after school on Thursday. "Hey, Billy," he said, "if you'll do me a favor, I'll do you one."

"You mean—the Saturday deal?" asked Billy, hoping Pete was going to back out of going to the deserted house.

Pete looked puzzled for a moment, then laughed. "Oh, *that*. I almost forgot about it."

Billy eyed him enviously. How could he forget about something so scary?

Pete kicked a pebble down the sidewalk. "I can't go this Saturday because I have to help my dad, but another time—" His voice trailed off.

"Yeah," said Billy quickly, "some other time." He was so relieved that their visit to the deserted house was postponed, he felt like shouting, "Hurrah!" But, of course, that wouldn't have sounded very brave.

Pete had his mind on something other than ghosts today. "It's my book report," he said miserably. "Miss Wilson says I have to have it finished by tomorrow, and I haven't even read the book yet."

Billy looked at the book Pete was carrying. *"Farmer Boy.* Oh, I've read that," he said quickly. "It's good."

"Not to me," said Pete. "I don't like to read. The only thing I like in school is arithmetic. If you write my report, I'll do your arithmetic."

Billy thought for a minute. It wouldn't take him long to write a report on *Farmer Boy,* not as long as doing his arithmetic would take. He'd have more time to play with Frisky.

"Okay," he said, "but we'll have to go to school early tomorrow so we can copy each other's papers. Miss Wilson knows our handwriting."

"I'll come at a quarter after eight," said Pete as he turned down his street. "See you!"

Billy worked on the book report as soon as he got home.

"Another book report so soon?" asked Aunt Kate pleasantly as she looked over his shoulder. "You do nice work, Billy."

Billy wondered what Aunt Kate would say if she knew he was writing the report for Pete and that he was going to copy Pete's arithmetic paper in return.

"She doesn't need to know," he told himself. "Nobody has to know." But Billy had the uneasy feeling that Somebody *did* know.

Because he finished his homework so promptly, Aunt Kate let Billy go over to see Uncle John after supper. Billy wanted to show him some new tricks he'd taught Frisky.

"Uncle John," he said as he burst into the older man's kitchen, "Frisky can roll over now and sit up when I tell him to. Look!"

Uncle John watched while Billy went through his tricks with Frisky. "Good dog," he said, patting Frisky's head. "You deserve a cookie. Bring one from the cookie jar, Billy, and have a couple yourself."

Billy ran for the cookies. Frisky jumped high and danced on his hind legs for his.

"Look!" cried Billy. "He can dance, too! Isn't he smart, Uncle John?"

Uncle John chuckled. "You bet he is! He's the smartest dog in this room!"

"He sure is!" exclaimed Billy.
Then he grinned sheepishly. "The
only dog in this room," he added as
Uncle John laughed.

"I believe he is learning to obey
you, Billy. And that's the important
thing for dogs to learn. Boys, too, by
the way."

"I try to be obedient," began Billy,
frowning a little.

"Good," said Uncle John, laying
his hand on the boy's shoulder.
"Jesus is in your life now, you know,
to help you be obedient and do what
is right."

Suddenly the book report and
arithmetic paper flashed into Billy's
mind. Should he tell Uncle John
what he and Pete were doing for

each other? But what if Uncle John told him he shouldn't do it? If he backed out now, Pete would be furious.

"I've got to go home, Uncle John," Billy said suddenly, picking up Frisky. "Good night."

Billy felt miserable as he ran across the yard to his own house.

7

Billy's Arithmetic Paper

Pete arrived at Billy's house promptly at 8:15 the next morning. The boys decided to do their copying in Billy's room instead of at school where Miss Wilson might see them.

Billy felt unhappy as he copied Pete's arithmetic paper. He felt even worse on his way to school and hardly heard Pete's talk about the tire swing his father was making for him.

"Pete doesn't seem to feel unhappy about cheating as I do," he told himself. "I wonder why. Is it because he's never received Jesus

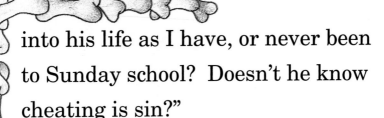

into his life as I have, or never been to Sunday school? Doesn't he know cheating is sin?"

"Hurry," urged Pete. "I hear the first bell." The boys broke into a run and reached the third-grade classroom just as the second bell rang.

Billy hung up his jacket and slipped into his seat. Miss Wilson made a few announcements before she started the arithmetic class.

"First, I'll collect your papers," she said, smiling pleasantly.

Billy felt terrible. His pounding heart seemed to say, "Cheat, cheat, cheat, cheat!" It sounded so loud to Billy that he wondered if anyone else could hear it. When Sally

handed him the papers from their row, he put his on top and handed them to the teacher.

Miss Wilson took the papers and put them on her desk, then went to the blackboard to explain the new lesson for the day.

Billy couldn't think. He couldn't answer when Miss Wilson called on him. He couldn't even remember seven times eight.

Finally arithmetic was over and Miss Wilson passed out the readers. Usually Billy loved reading, but not today. He read the same page over three times before he knew what it said. He had a hard time answering the questions at the end of the story, too.

Oh, if only he could stop feeling miserable and be happy again! Then he remembered what Uncle John had told him to do if he did wrong.

"Tell God what you've done, Billy, and ask His forgiveness."

Billy closed his eyes behind his open book and prayed, "Jesus, forgive me for cheating. I won't do it again. I promise." Billy waited with his eyes closed, waited for the awful feeling to go away, but it didn't. Something was still wrong. The arithmetic paper—he had to tell Miss Wilson he had copied it.

"I can't," he told himself. "Never, never!"

Uncle John's words of the night before came back to him: "Jesus is in your life now to help you do what is right."

But how could he tell Miss Wilson that he had cheated?

The bell rang for recess. The boys and girls scrambled for their jackets and ran outside to play. Billy didn't feel like joining them. He had to tell Miss Wilson what he had done, but how could he? "Jesus, help me," he pleaded silently as he stood up and dragged his unwilling feet to her desk.

"Miss Wilson," said Billy, fighting back the tears, "that arithmetic paper I handed in this morning—I copied it. I didn't do it myself. I—I

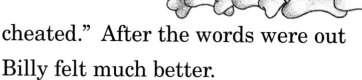

cheated." After the words were out Billy felt much better.

Miss Wilson was very kind. She thanked Billy for telling her. She said she would give him another chance to do the lesson since she knew he was really sorry. She was sure he wouldn't cheat again.

Billy was still talking to Miss Wilson when the children came back from the playground after recess was over. Pete looked at him curiously. It wasn't like Billy to stay in during recess.

On the way home for lunch, Pete caught up with Billy. "What were you talking to Miss Wilson about at recess?" he demanded with a scowl. "You didn't tell on me, did you?"

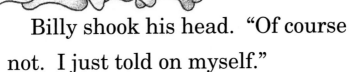

Billy shook his head. "Of course not. I just told on myself."

Pete stopped walking and stared at Billy. "You—you're kidding!"

Billy shook his head. "No, I'm not. I—I had to, Pete."

"Had to?" Pete almost shouted. "What d'you mean?"

Billy's heart started to pound. He'd been wanting to tell Pete about Jesus, but now that he had the chance he felt tongue-tied.

Pete wanted an answer. Billy groped for words. "I belong to God now, Pete. Jesus came into my life, and—well, I can't do things like cheating. I mean—I don't want to. I'm—I'm a Christian."

"Christian! What do you mean?" asked Pete a little scornfully. Suddenly Billy remembered the little picture Uncle John drew to explain it to him some months ago. He felt in his pocket for a pencil. He found a little scrap of paper, too.

"It's like this," he said, squatting down on the sidewalk so he could make the lines straighter. Pete squatted beside him.

"God is up here_____

and we're down here_____
and the only One who can bring us together is Jesus, because He died on the cross to pay for our sins."

Billy drew a cross between the two lines.

"When a person takes Jesus as his Savior, Jesus takes away his sin and comes to be with him forever. Jesus helps him be good."

"I don't get it," Pete said, getting to his feet.

"If you'd go to Sunday school with me or talk to Uncle John—" began Billy.

"Naw, I don't want to."

They started walking again. Finally Pete spoke.

"If you're dumb enough to tell on yourself, go ahead, but don't you dare tell on me." He scowled at Billy.

"I won't," said Billy, "but I won't write any more book reports for you either." Billy was surprised at his courage. He'd never dared stand up to Pete before. Jesus was helping him do lots of hard things today.

Pete turned down his own street without a word, and Billy ran the rest of the way home. Or did he float? He was so happy he wasn't sure.

8

A Missing Pup

Dad had come home for a few
days and gone again. Billy wistfully
remembered the good time they'd
had. Even Aunt Kate laughed, and
not once had she scolded Frisky,
unless she did it when Billy wasn't
listening. But ever since Frisky had
discovered the mouse, which they
later caught in the trap, Aunt Kate
hadn't suggested getting rid of him.

But one day when Billy came
home from school for lunch he found
Aunt Kate with an unhappy look on
her face again. She was untangling
her yarn and rolling it into a ball.

Billy's heart sank. What had happened? Aunt Kate didn't wait long to tell him.

"I left my knitting for about three minutes while I answered the doorbell, and when I came back, you should have seen the mess! Yes, it was your dog. I had to take out row after row, and I've been all morning trying to untangle the yarn."

Billy looked miserably from the tangled yarn to his pup lying curled up in a ball in the corner fast asleep. If only Frisky didn't get into so much trouble! Not that he meant to. He was just frisky.

"Shall I help you untangle it?" he ventured timidly.

Aunt Kate shook her head. "Never mind. I'll do it myself. You just eat your lunch and get back to school."

Billy sat down at the table to eat, but somehow his peanut butter sandwiches didn't taste very good today. He saw the mailman pass the window and jumped up. Maybe there would be a letter from Dad. If ever he wanted a letter it was today.

"Yes, I think I have a letter for you, young man," said the short, squat mailman pleasantly, searching in his mailbag. "Here it is, and one for your aunt."

Billy looked at the two envelopes, both with the same handwriting. He ran in, tore open his own, and handed the other one to Aunt Kate.

"One for me?" she asked in surprise.

Billy read the letter while he finished his sandwiches. "Daddy said he might come home next week," he announced gleefully, forgetting to wait until his mouth was empty.

"I know," answered Aunt Kate quietly. She was smiling, and her eyes were shining. She seemed to have forgotten about Frisky and the yarn.

Billy looked at Aunt Kate curiously. Sometimes she was very hard to understand.

The clock said 12:30. Time to get back to school. He'd better hurry, or he'd be late. Frisky followed him to the door.

"No, Frisky, you can't come," Billy said, pushing him back gently. "You might get lost if you run around alone. I'll be back pretty soon." He shut the door firmly.

Billy heard the bell ring when he was still half a block away from school. He ran as fast as he could. Just as he opened the big front door of the school, he looked back. He could see a small dog running down the street toward the school. It looked just like Frisky, but it couldn't be. He had shut the door tightly when he left. "Somebody else's pup, I guess," he murmured as he hurried into his room.

Billy thought about stopping in to see Uncle John on his way home from school that afternoon but decided he had better check on Frisky first. Aunt Kate, not Frisky, met him at the door.

"Billy," she began as soon as he had come in, "did you see your dog on your way home from school?"

Billy shook his head. "Isn't he here? I didn't let him out."

"I didn't either," Aunt Kate went on. "At least I didn't mean to, but right after you left an insurance man came. I opened the door to talk to him and Frisky ran out between our legs—so fast I couldn't catch him. He ran after you in the direction of the school, so I thought maybe—" Her voice trailed off.

"I did see a pup," answered Billy slowly, "just as I went into school, but I didn't think it was Frisky."

"Maybe if you look around the neighborhood you will find him,"

76

suggested Aunt Kate. "I'm sorry he got away, but I had no idea he would dart out like that."

"I know, Aunt Kate. He's awfully hard to catch, but I'll find him. I'll look for him right now."

"Here, take a couple of cookies," suggested Aunt Kate. "I made your favorite ones, chocolate with frosting."

Billy took the cookies and murmured his thanks. But how could he care about cookies today when his pup was missing?

9
A Special Verse

Billy trudged up and down the streets of the neighborhood, calling Frisky, and asking everyone he met if they had seen his pup, but nobody had. By the time he reached home he was so close to tears he didn't trust himself to speak to anyone. He hoped he could get to his room without Aunt Kate seeing him. But he couldn't. She was sitting in the kitchen waiting. She stood up when Billy came in, went over to him, and put her hands on his shoulders.

"Didn't you find him, Billy?" she asked gently.

Billy shook his head, trying hard to keep the tears back.

"Don't worry. I think he'll show up. Come on and have some supper."

Billy didn't feel like eating supper when Frisky was lost, but he sat down at the table anyway.

Aunt Kate brought the food to the table. What was that good smell? Billy looked up quickly and smiled a little crooked smile through his tears. Hot dogs! Aunt Kate had made his favorite meal!

"I bought some pop at the corner store," she said. "It's not very nutritious, but if you drink a glass of milk before you go to bed—"

"Oh I will," Billy assured her quickly.

Billy was putting catsup on his hot dog when Aunt Kate said, "Billy, I was noticing the net you use when you play basketball by the garage. It has a hole in the bottom. If you would like to have me fix it for you, I could sew it up in a jiffy. I don't suppose you like it torn like that."

Billy's mouth fell open, and he dropped his eyes to his plate so Aunt Kate wouldn't see the laughter in them. Who ever heard of a sewed-up basket for basketball? But he couldn't laugh at Aunt Kate, not when she was trying so hard to be nice.

"It's not torn, Aunt Kate," he managed finally. "That's the way it's supposed to be so the ball can come back down."

Aunt Kate began to giggle. Billy was glad he could laugh, too.

"Well, if I'm not a stupid old aunt!" she exclaimed. "It's a good thing I didn't fix it as a surprise as I was planning. In the small town in Canada where I came from we didn't have a gym for basketball. I've watched a lot of hockey games, though, and wouldn't make any silly mistakes on those rules."

"Tell me about hockey, Aunt Kate," said Billy, finding himself interested. "Then I'll tell you about basketball."

After they talked about hockey and basketball, Aunt Kate told Billy about her life on the Canadian prairies when she was a little girl. Billy

was so interested he forgot for a little while that Frisky was lost.

"Oh, my," said Aunt Kate at last, jumping up from the table. "Look at the clock! It's time I did dishes and you did your homework."

"I don't have any homework, Aunt Kate," began Billy. "May I run over to talk to Uncle John for a little while?"

"Oh, I don't think—" began Aunt Kate, then changed her mind. "I guess it would be all right. But just for a few minutes. It's almost bed-time, you know."

Billy was glad he could talk to Uncle John. He told him all about Frisky's being gone since noon and how he had looked and looked but hadn't found him. He even told Uncle John about Aunt Kate making his favorite cookies and fixing hot dogs and pop for supper.

"And Uncle John," he added, breaking into a grin, "you'd never guess what Aunt Kate wanted to do to my basketball net!"

Uncle John shook his head. "I give up," he said.

"Sew it up!" exclaimed Billy, beginning to laugh. "She thought it was torn!"

"Ho, ho, ho!" laughed Uncle John, slapping his knee and holding his sides. "Ho, ho, ho! Women are funny!"

Billy and Uncle John laughed so hard they had to wipe their eyes.

"I'd better go home now, Uncle John," said Billy at last. "Aunt Kate said I shouldn't stay long."

Uncle John stood up and put his hand on Billy's shoulder. "Before you go, let's say our special verse," he said. "'We know that all things work together for good to them that love God.' Come on, say it with me this time."

Billy repeated the words with Uncle John. Strange how they made him feel better about everything!

"And now let's pray together that the Lord will take care of Frisky wherever he is tonight," said Uncle John.

While Uncle John prayed, a couple of tears squeezed out of Billy's eyes and splashed on his folded hands. He wiped them off quickly on his trousers so Uncle John wouldn't notice. After all, didn't the Bible say God worked things out for those who loved Him? That must mean even things like lost puppies!

As Billy raced across the yard to his own house, he decided to tell Aunt Kate about his special verse. She had been so nice since Frisky got lost.

"Aunt Kate!" he called when he didn't find her in the kitchen or living room.

"Just a minute," she answered from her bedroom.

It was more than a minute before Aunt Kate appeared in her yellow housecoat. Billy stared at her. She looked as if she had been crying. For an instant he wished he hadn't called her.

"What is it, Billy?" she prompted, coming to where he stood by his bedroom door.

"It's—it's just a verse, Aunt Kate," Billy began fingering the doorknob, "one that Uncle John taught me. Shall I say it for you?"

"Certainly."

"'We know that all things work together for good to them that love God,'" quoted Billy, but he had the feeling Aunt Kate wasn't really listening.

Aunt Kate put her hand on Billy's shoulder. "What was that, Billy? Say it again."

Billy repeated the words.

Aunt Kate dropped her hand and stared off into space for a few moments as if she had forgotten that Billy was there. Billy squirmed, waiting for her to say something, but she didn't. Finally he took a deep breath.

"It's a verse for lost puppies and for—"

"All things," finished Aunt Kate. "All things," she said again softly. "I haven't thought of that verse for years."

"Uncle John says it really works," added Billy earnestly.

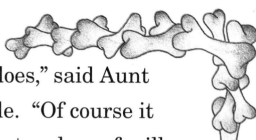

"Of course it does," said Aunt Kate with a smile. "Of course it does. Now you get a glass of milk and hurry off to bed."

10
The Newspaper Ad

Billy couldn't keep his mind on his school work the next day. Where was Frisky? Was he lost in the woods? Had somebody stolen him? Had somebody run over him with a car? Oh, no! Billy wouldn't even think about anything so awful. He must only be lost in the woods. Right after school he would go to look for him.

Billy didn't go outside for recess. He just sat in his seat and stared out the window, thinking of Frisky.

"What's the matter, Billy?" asked Miss Wilson. "Why don't you go and play with the other children?"

Billy told his teacher the whole sad story. She patted him on the shoulder and said, "Don't worry, Billy, you'll probably find him. Have you looked in the lost-and-found column in the newspaper? Maybe someone has found him and is waiting for you to claim him."

"Maybe so," echoed Billy, excited at the thought. "I'll be sure to look in tonight's paper."

At last school was over. Billy grabbed his jacket and hurried to the front door. A gust of wind almost blew him over, and cold rain slapped his face. "I'd better go look

for Frisky before I go home," he told himself. "If I go home first, Aunt Kate will say the weather is too bad."

A familiar honk came from across the street. Billy's heart sank. There was Aunt Kate now. Reluctantly he ran to the car.

"Get in quickly, Billy," she said. "This storm came up so suddenly that I knew you'd get soaked if you walked. I believe you are already. You'll have to get into some dry things as soon as we get home."

Aunt Kate didn't mention Frisky. Billy knew it was no use to ask if he could go to look for him in this weather. Probably Aunt Kate didn't care that Frisky was lost, anyway.

Maybe she was glad. Billy glanced at his aunt sideways. Yes, she probably was glad that Frisky was lost so she wouldn't have any more trouble with him. Billy felt alone and miserable again.

"Here we are, Billy," said Aunt Kate. "Run as quickly as you can and hold the door open for me."

After Billy had changed to dry clothes he sat looking sadly out the window. If Frisky were in the woods he'd be all wet by now, and scared, too. Was he someplace crying for Billy?

He suddenly remembered what Miss Wilson had said about looking in the paper. "It should be here soon," he murmured.

At last a car stopped out in front. Billy saw the paper boy get out and run to their door. He ran to get the paper from him. As he spread it out on the floor, a headline caught his eye: "Patient From Mental Hospital Escapes."

"Guess people run away, too," he murmured as he turned to the want ads and the lost-and-found section.

Found: a black leather purse on Main Street yesterday. Owner please call 336-2784.

Found: a watch—

Billy didn't bother to read the rest. No puppy had been found, and

that was all that mattered. His eyes
drifted to the next column.

Lost: a small,
black-and-white
puppy answering
to the name,
Frisky, lost on
Walnut Street
yesterday after-
noon.

Billy grabbed the paper and ran
to find his aunt. "Look, Aunt Kate,"
he shouted. "Somebody else lost a
pup just like ours. His name is
Frisky, too!"

Aunt Kate smiled. "Really?
What's the phone number?"

Billy read the number slowly,
"336-7285." He frowned thought-

fully. "Why, that's our number, Aunt Kate. W-what?"

"I put the ad in yesterday afternoon as soon as I knew Frisky was lost." Her eyes twinkled. "Maybe we'll get a call from somebody."

Billy smiled up at her. "Thanks, Aunt Kate," he said. He walked slowly back to the living room with the paper. He couldn't believe it. Aunt Kate put an ad in the paper to help him find Frisky. She did care, after all! Now, if the phone would only ring and somebody say they had found him.

A huge moving van pulled up in front of the house next door. Billy watched with interest as the men began to unload it.

"Looks like we have new neighbors," commented Aunt Kate, coming in from the kitchen. "What a day to be moving!" She picked up the newspaper Billy had dropped, sat down in the rocker, and began to read it.

"I wonder if they have a boy my age," mused Billy aloud. "I hope so. There must be a baby, because there's a highchair." Billy watched the men carry chairs, tables, beds, boxes, and bundles to the house. He was still looking when a car drove up. Out stepped a man, a woman with a baby in her arms, and a small boy.

"Look, Aunt Kate," he called. "There they are—our new neigh-

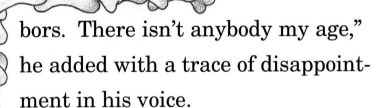

bors. There isn't anybody my age," he added with a trace of disappointment in his voice.

Aunt Kate came to the window to look. "I'll have to take some cookies over in a day or two," she said, "and get acquainted. By the way, Billy, listen to what it says here in the paper: 'Dogs unattended found running in the streets will be taken by the dogcatcher to the dog pound. Owners may claim them by paying the fine of ten dollars.' "

"Oh, Aunt Kate," cried Billy, "do you think the dogcatcher could have found Frisky?"

"Why don't I call the pound and ask?" suggested Aunt Kate.

Billy followed her into the kitchen. He waited breathlessly while she dialed the number.

"Do you by any chance have a small black-and-white rat terrier at the pound?" asked Aunt Kate when she had made the connection.

Billy's heart almost stopped beating. He strained his ears to hear what the man was saying. Aunt Kate was nodding her head. "I see. Yes, I realize that. We'll be down in a few minutes to check. I see. Thank you very much."

"What did he say?" asked Billy even before Aunt Kate had hung up the receiver.

"There are several black-and-white terriers at the pound. One could be

Frisky, but he's not sure."

"Can we go see, Aunt Kate?" Billy was so excited he almost shouted.

Aunt Kate smiled. "I'm ready. Go get your jacket and cap."

At the door Billy turned. He had just thought of something. "It costs ten dollars, doesn't it, Aunt Kate? I don't have that much money."

Aunt Kate laughed. "Never mind, Billy. I was the one who let him out, so I will pay the bill."

Right at that minute Billy thought Aunt Kate was the most wonderful aunt that had ever lived. He ran to get his jacket and joined her in the car.

When they reached the pound, Billy ran ahead of Aunt Kate.

"There he is! There he is!" he shouted.

Sure enough, Frisky was jumping up at the bars, straining to get to his master. In a minute the black-and-white puppy was scrambling into Billy's arms, and Aunt Kate was handing the man a ten-dollar bill.

11

More Trouble Ahead

One day Aunt Kate picked Billy
up after school on her way home
from town. Billy jumped into the
car, then stared at his aunt. Her
hair—it was different—pretty and
puffy like Mother's used to be.

"Your hair looks pretty, Aunt
Kate," he said.

Aunt Kate laughed. She had
been smiling and laughing a lot
lately. Billy had, too. Frisky had
been found, and Daddy was coming
home tomorrow.

"There's Mrs. Parker ringing our
front doorbell," remarked Aunt Kate

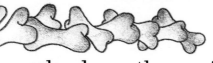

as she drove the car into the drive-way. "And she has her two children with her. Billy, you bring in the packages, and I'll let her in."

Billy came in just in time to hear a woman's high-pitched voice say-ing, "Oh, a nasty dog! Get down! Get away from me!" Then a baby began to cry.

Aunt Kate came shooing Frisky in front of her. "Put him in the basement while they're here," she said quietly. "They probably won't stay long."

Frisky put his tail between his legs and slunk down the stairs after his master.

"Poor Frisky," said Billy, giving him a pat. "You didn't mean anything, but some ladies are funny about dogs."

He felt as if he should stay with Frisky to cheer him up, but something made him want to go upstairs and hear what the new neighbor was saying. At the living room door he stopped short.

"A dog is a terrible nuisance. At the last place we lived, the neighbors signed a petition for a no-dog neighborhood. We all had such lovely yards and didn't want to worry about our flower beds being dug up. Now Jimmy is old enough to play outside alone, and I certainly wouldn't want him frightened or bitten by a dog!"

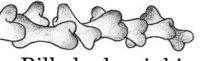

Billy had a sinking feeling in the pit of his stomach. Mechanically he listened to Aunt Kate's answer.

"Billy's dog wouldn't bite anyone, Mrs. Parker. You don't need to worry about your flowers, either. Billy will keep him out of your yard." She paused. "I'm glad you liked the cookies I sent over. Could I make you a cup of tea?"

"No thank you," came the answer. "I must get home and start supper. My husband comes home early. But I did want to return your plate."

"Well, do come again when you can stay awhile," said Aunt Kate, following the woman and her children to the front door.

Billy poked his head around the corner and peered after them. What a cranky neighbor! Just when Aunt Kate was beginning to like Frisky, a neighbor like that had to move in. Billy had an uneasy feeling that there was trouble ahead for Frisky.

Just then Pete came pedaling down the street on his bike. Billy ran to talk to him. He could tell by the look in Pete's eyes that he was up to something.

"How about going to the deserted house with me tomorrow?" he asked in a low voice.

That scared feeling came over Billy again, starting at the top of his head and going down into his toes. He just didn't feel ready for a meet-

ing with Old Man Hitchcock's ghost. Suddenly he remembered something.

"My dad's coming home tomorrow, so I can't go. I haven't seen him for a long time."

"You don't want to go," accused Pete.

"Yes, I do," answered Billy quickly.

"You're scared."

"I'm not either."

Billy hated having anyone think he was scared, especially Pete. He had to prove to Pete he was as brave as he was. "School's out next Friday. Why don't we go then?"

"Friday?" Pete screwed up his face thoughtfully as if he were an

important person who had lots of business to attend to on Fridays. Billy waited tensely, almost hoping he'd say he was too busy.

"Friday is okay, I guess," Pete said. "See ya'." And he pedaled away.

Billy looked over his shoulder as he ran into the house. He had the queer feeling that a ghost was chasing him.

"Silly," he told himself, "ghosts come out only at night." But hadn't Sid McClennan seen Old Man Hitchcock's ghost in the daytime? Billy closed the door behind him and shivered a little.

Frisky came bounding up to him, begging to play. Billy forgot about

ghosts and deserted houses as he
ran to the basement with his pup at
his heels. Next Friday was a whole
week away. Lots of things could
change before then. He threw the
ball, and Frisky chased it.

"Daddy!" shrieked Billy, running out of the house and flinging himself into his father's arms. Billy didn't realize how much he had missed his father until he felt his strong arms around him.

Aunt Kate came out, too, to join in the happy reunion. Billy noticed she had on a pretty blue dress, and her hair was soft and fluffy around her face.

"I'll help you with your suitcases, Daddy," offered Billy, then stopped short. Frisky had bounded out of the house unnoticed and was nosing

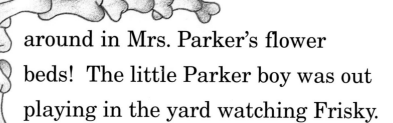

around in Mrs. Parker's flower
beds! The little Parker boy was out
playing in the yard watching Frisky.

Billy dropped Dad's suitcase and
ran, but he was too late. An angry
Mrs. Parker reached Frisky first.

"Ruining my flowers!" she sput-
tered. "Get that pesky dog out of
my yard and away from my child!"
Raising her foot, she gave Frisky a
kick. He ran yelping home with an
indignant Billy running after him.

Gathering the trembling pup into
his arms, Billy tried to soothe him.
"Don't cry, Frisky. She's mean, but I
won't let her kick you again. You
have to stay out of her yard. She'll
call the dogcatcher and—" Billy felt

so sad that he couldn't finish the sentence.

Dad twirled his mustache thoughtfully when Billy told him about it. "We'll have to get a long chain for Frisky," he said. "Of course he wants to run outside every chance he gets in this nice weather. We'll chain him to the clothesline, and Mrs. Parker won't have a thing to be cross about. Tomorrow morning I'll pick up a chain when I go to town."

"I'm so glad you're home, Daddy," said Billy, throwing his arms around his father's neck.

"So am I, son," answered Dad. "I'm getting tired of being away from you so much. I may have a chance to get a job with my company right here in Burlingham. How would you like that?"

"I'd like that fine, Daddy," answered Billy. Then he thought of something. If Dad got a job in Burlingham like he had before, Aunt Kate wouldn't need to stay with them anymore. Suddenly Billy knew that he wanted Aunt Kate to stay with them—almost as much as he wanted Dad not to go away on trips. He looked across the room at her. She had such a happy smile on her face. Do you suppose she was happy because maybe she wouldn't have to take care of Billy and Frisky much longer? Thinking about that made Billy feel a little sad.

The next day Dad fixed up the chain for Frisky. At first Frisky didn't like being tied up, but soon he found out he could run a long way if he pulled the chain along the clothesline. He had fun chasing butterflies, growling at birds, and just lying in the warm May sunshine. When Billy came home from school, he untied Frisky and let him run freely around the yard for a while under his watchful eye.

Jimmy Parker learned to love Frisky, too. Every time he came outside to play he would toddle over to Billy's yard to pet the pup. Frisky seemed to know he must be gentle with the little fellow. He ran in circles and barked to make him

laugh. He licked the boy's hands and sometimes his face, but he never tried to bite.

Mrs. Parker didn't want Jimmy playing with Frisky. "Think of all the germs he's picking up," she said when Billy went over to say he was sorry Frisky had played in her flower beds. "What if he gets bitten? I think we should rid the neighborhood of these pesky dogs. I just can't keep Jimmy away from them!"

"Maybe you could put up a fence," suggested Billy.

"We can't afford to put up a fence!" retorted the woman. "Fences cost more than you think! Besides, your dog's barking bothers me. He even wakes up my baby, sometimes."

Billy's heart sank. He talked to Aunt Kate about it, but she didn't know what to do. Even Uncle John had no solution this time. He told Billy to pray about it and to remember the verse. Hadn't it worked before?

Yes, Billy had to agree. Even losing Frisky had worked out for the best. He had found out what Aunt Kate was really like, and Aunt Kate had seemed to change her mind about Frisky around that time, too.

"We know that all things work together for good to them that love God," he repeated as he threw a stick for Frisky to run after. Any-

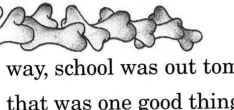

way, school was out tomorrow and that was one good thing. Maybe if he was home all the time, he could watch Frisky better and keep him from being a nuisance to Mrs. Parker. At least he would try.

Billy and Pete Explore

Billy felt wonderful! School was over for three whole months! He raced home to celebrate with Frisky.

"School's over, Aunt Kate," he shouted as he ran into the house to change his clothes. " 'No more classrooms, no more books, no more teachers' dirty looks!' " he sang.

Aunt Kate came out of her bedroom all dressed up. "You should be thankful you have a school to go to, Billy," she said, but she smiled as she said it.

"Going some place?" asked Billy, thinking his Aunt Kate was getting prettier every day.

"Yes, to a missionary luncheon at church. I made you a sack lunch. Thought you might like to eat outside today."

"Oh, boy!" Billy exclaimed. "Frisky and I will go exploring. Okay, Aunt Kate?"

"I suppose, but be careful, and don't stay away too long." She leaned over and gave Billy a quick kiss on the cheek. "I'll be back around four o'clock, I think."

Billy changed into his old clothes as quickly as possible, grabbed his sack lunch, and hurried out to untie Frisky. The pup raced around the yard, delighted to be free.

Billy ran around the yard with him until he was tired. Panting from the exercise, he threw himself on the ground to rest. Frisky jumped up on him and licked his face.

Billy laughed. "Don't you know you're giving me all kinds of germs, Frisky?" he said. "At least that's what Mrs. Parker says."

Frisky only jumped up and licked him some more. Billy gathered the dog into his arms and looked up at the patches of blue sky he could see through the maple trees. He felt close to God as he watched the sunlight dance through the leafy branches. Yes, God had made everything work out with Aunt Kate. "But there's still Mrs. Parker, God," he worried aloud. "Will you please

make her move away or something, so she won't make trouble for Frisky?"

"Hi, Billy!"

Billy sat up quickly. Pete was running across the yard toward him. He flopped down on the grass beside Billy.

"Today's the day," he said, picking a blade of grass to chew. "Remember? Or have you changed your mind about going to the deserted house?"

Billy shook his head. "Not me. Unless you'd—rather not." He didn't mention that he'd been hoping Pete would change his mind about going today.

"You scared?"

Billy shook his head. "Are you?"

"Nope, let's go."

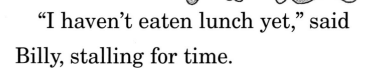

"I haven't eaten lunch yet," said Billy, stalling for time.

"You can eat it on the way. Come on."

Billy munched a peanut-butter sandwich as he started off for the edge of town with Pete. Frisky scampered and sniffed alongside them, sometimes running off on little side trips of his own.

The sun was shining so brightly, and it was such a good feeling to know that school was out for the summer, that Billy forgot to feel afraid until the Stony Creek deserted house loomed into view.

"There it is, Pete," he said in a thin, scared voice. Pete gave him a quick glance.

Billy had to act brave even if he didn't feel like it. "Come on," he said, leading the way through the underbrush and tall grass around the house.

The front door wouldn't open, but the boys crawled through a window that had lost its glass. At first Billy moved around cautiously, half expecting something to jump out and grab him, but the sun shining through the broken windows so warm and friendly made him forget about ghosts. It was such fun to explore the old house!

"Hey, come see this saddle!" called Pete from the room behind the kitchen.

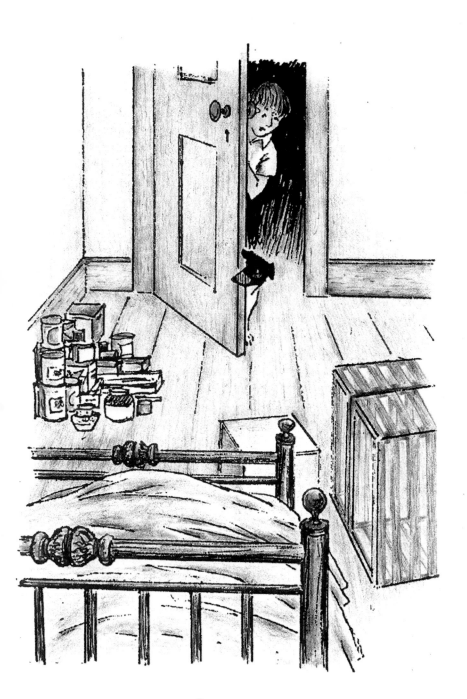

Billy left the pile of old magazines he was looking through and ran to find Pete. On the way he spied a stairway.

"Hey! Pete, come on upstairs!" he yelled. Frisky bounded up the stairs ahead of Billy with Pete trailing behind.

The first room they peered into didn't have anything in it but an old broken-down dresser. Cobwebs hung from the ceiling, and dust lay thick on the floor.

Billy wandered down the hall to the next door. This one was closed. He turned the knob, opened it, and walked in. Billy's mouth dropped open. In one corner of the room was an old bed with some quilts on it.

Two wooden boxes were stacked together to make a table and another one a chair. Against the wall were stacked cans of food, boxes of crackers, and cigarettes.

Billy felt shivers go up and down his spine. Old Sid had been right after all. There was somebody living in the deserted house.

Frisky was busily sniffing around the cans of food. Billy grabbed him and ran out of the room. He had to tell Pete about his discovery, and then they had better get out of here.

Billy almost bumped into Pete coming down the hall. He grabbed Pete's arm. "I found a—a hideout," he said in a hoarse whisper, glancing uneasily behind him. "Somebody

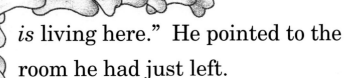

is living here." He pointed to the room he had just left.

Pete stuck his head in the door, took a good look, and then closed the door quickly. He didn't argue with Billy about leaving the deserted house. They ran down the stairs with Frisky at their heels and jumped out of the window through which they had entered. Not until they were a safe distance down the road did they speak. Then it was Billy who broke the silence.

"Ghosts don't eat, do they, Pete?" he said. "Or sleep in beds?"

Pete looked worried. "I dunno," he said with a shrug.

"Maybe I should ask Uncle John," suggested Billy.

Pete shook his head. "Don't," he said. "Let's not tell anybody about what we discovered. And some-day—let's go back."

Billy shivered even though the sunshine felt warm on his back. "Sure," he answered bravely. "Someday."

Right now "someday" seemed safely far away.

14

A Strange Man

As Billy had hoped, Dad came home to stay.

"You mean you don't have to travel any more?" asked Billy unbelievingly.

"Oh, once in a while, but most of the time I'll be home as I used to be. What do you think of that?"

"I think it's great, Dad," answered Billy. "But what about Aunt Kate? Will she leave now?"

A frown replaced the smile on Dad's face. "Billy," he said seriously, twitching his nose and twirling his mustache, "I hoped that by now you would have grown fond of Aunt Kate as she has for you. Couldn't you try—?"

"But I *do* like her, Dad," Billy almost shouted. "I don't want her to leave. I want you to stay home, but I want Aunt Kate to stay here, too, and I was afraid—"

"That you couldn't have us both," finished Dad. He was smiling again. "I think it's time we had a good old tussle," he said, grabbing Billy's shoulders.

In a moment they were both on the floor, wrestling and laughing. Frisky was so excited that he jumped all around them barking so loudly Aunt Kate came running. She clapped her hands over her ears.

"What a commotion! Frisky, stop your barking!"

Dad got up from the floor with a sheepish look on his face, brushing off his trousers. Billy stayed on the floor and rolled around with Frisky for a minute. Suddenly Billy wondered if Aunt Kate might be angry. She hated barking. He glanced up quickly. To his surprise Aunt Kate and Dad were standing together watching Billy and Frisky. They were both smiling, and Dad had his arm around Aunt Kate.

Billy stood to his feet and stared. Aunt Kate blushed and pulled away from Dad. "The picnic supper is ready," she said. "When do we go?"

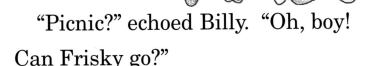

"Picnic?" echoed Billy. "Oh, boy! Can Frisky go?"

"If you take his chain along," answered Dad. "You'd better run over and tell Uncle John we are ready."

"Uncle John, too? Oh, boy!" Billy raced to the house across the yard, Frisky following at his heels.

They were just finishing Aunt Kate's delicious apple pie at the park an hour later when a strange-looking man wandered past their picnic table. Billy looked at him curiously. His trousers were too big and his shirt too small. Brown, curly hair stuck out in every direction from under the cap that was pulled down over his eyes. Maybe it was the way he walked that was the

strangest of all, so quickly one minute as if he had important business to tend to, and slowly the next, as if he had forgotten all about his important business.

"I wonder who that man could be," mused Aunt Kate. "He looks strange."

Dad laughed. "You had better quit looking at other men, strange or not," he teased. He winked at Uncle John, and Aunt Kate blushed. Puzzled, Billy scratched his head.

"Why don't we take Frisky for a little walk," suggested Uncle John. "Otherwise we might find ourselves on the clean-up committee."

"I'll wash the plates," announced Dad.

"You can't wash paper plates," Billy said with a grin.

"That's why I volunteered," said Dad, twirling the end of his mustache.

Billy had a jumble of thoughts in his head as he started off through the park with Frisky and Uncle John. It was fun having Dad so jolly and Aunt Kate so smiley, but he didn't always understand what they were laughing about.

Should he tell Uncle John about what he and Pete had found in the deserted house? No, he'd better not. Pete had told him to keep it a secret.

"A penny for your thoughts," remarked Uncle John when they had walked along in silence for a few minutes.

Billy gave Uncle John a sidelong glance. "Guess I'm not thinking about much of anything," he answered, feeling uncomfortable. Then, to change the subject, "Uncle John, there's that strange man again."

Sure enough, the man that had passed their picnic table was sitting on the grass with his back against a big tree. Frisky growled and strained on his leash.

"What's so strange about him?" asked Uncle John.

"Well, he's not doing anything, just sitting there—" Billy's voice trailed off.

"I reckon he's holding up that tree," answered Uncle John with a chuckle. "Besides, he's probably watching the squirrels, or maybe just thinking. Nothing wrong with that, is there?"

"N—no," admitted Billy slowly. But what was there about the man that made him feel uneasy?

"Too bad your Aunt Kate is such a good cook," sighed Uncle John, rubbing his stomach. "I ate too much. It all tasted so good after my bachelor meals."

"You're a good cook, too, Uncle John," insisted Billy loyally. "Remember that time we went camping and you made hobo stew? I wish we could go again."

"We will," promised Uncle John. "We will. I think there are some plans in the making right now."

"What plans?" pressed Billy, but Uncle John would tell him no more.

"Wait and see, Billy," was all he would say.

15

MISSING!

Where Is Jimmy?

The soft summer breeze cooled Billy's hot face as he coasted down the street on his bike. He was tired after the Little League game, but happy. "We really smeared them," he said to himself as he guided the bike into his driveway. "I only struck out once this time and got two one-base hits, then walked the rest of the time." He could hardly wait to tell Aunt Kate. He glanced up at the basketball net as he parked his bike. If Aunt Kate didn't know any more about baseball than basketball, she wouldn't even know what one-base hits were, he thought, his face twisting into a grin.

"Aunt Kate," he called as he burst into the back door. But there was no answer. "Wonder where Aunt Kate is," he mused.

Last night's newspaper was spread out on the kitchen table. Billy suddenly remembered he hadn't read the comics the night before. As he turned the page, a headline caught his eye: "Escapee from Mental Hospital Still on the Loose." He shivered. "I'm glad Dad is home nights now," he murmured.

Billy finished the comics and ran outside. Where was Aunt Kate? He was hungry. He glanced over at the

Parker's house. Was that a police car in front of their place?

It certainly was, and that was a police officer at the door. Mrs. Parker was coming out of the house now followed by her husband and Aunt Kate. Mrs. Parker was crying.

"He was right here a few minutes ago, officer," she said. "I can't understand it. He's never run off before."

"We'll have a search party organized in no time," Billy heard the officer say, "and it won't be long until we find your boy. Mr. Parker, you may come with me."

"Aunt Kate, is Jimmy lost?" asked Billy in a hoarse whisper as the officer and Mr. Parker were leaving.

Aunt Kate nodded.

"Could I go and help look for him?" asked Billy.

"I'm afraid not," answered Aunt Kate. "You run home and get my knitting basket, will you? I'm going to stay with Mrs. Parker and might just as well knit as sit idle."

Billy felt a little insulted as he turned to go for the knitting basket. Why couldn't he look for Jimmy, too? He was returning to the Parker house with Aunt Kate's knitting basket in his hand when Frisky attracted his attention. The pup was wriggling at the end of his chain, longing to get loose. An idea flashed into Billy's mind.

"Wait a minute, Frisky. I'll be right back," he promised.

Aunt Kate thanked him for bringing the basket. "Make yourself a sandwich," she said, "and pray for Jimmy's safety. Remember how you felt when Frisky was lost."

Yes, Billy remembered. That's why he was going to try to do something about Jimmy's being lost. And Frisky was going to do something, too! Billy closed the kitchen door carefully and looked around the small entryway. Sure enough, there was Jimmy's jacket. He hadn't worn it today because the weather was so warm.

"Please, God, make it work," he prayed as he put the jacket under

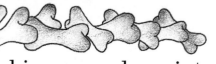

his arm and ran into his own house to call Pete.

"Pete," Billy said breathlessly over the phone, "want to do some detective work with me?"

"Sure."

"The little boy next door is lost. You and I and Frisky can be a search party to try to find him. Maybe Frisky will be able to track him down. He's an awfully smart pup."

"I'll be right over," answered Pete.

In a few minutes Pete rode into the yard on his bike. Together Billy and Pete ran to the clothesline to release Frisky.

Billy held Jimmy's jacket up to Frisky's nose. Frisky sniffed it,

then began running around the
yard in circles, excited to be free
from his chain.

"Here Frisky," called Billy. "Come
here and smell the jacket. Find
Jimmy. Show us where to go."

Frisky sniffed the jacket, then
ran more circles around the boys.

Billy was disappointed. "He's just
a pup. I guess he doesn't know how
to track anybody down." He looked
at Pete, unsure of what to do next.

"Smart detectives don't need dogs
to help them," said Pete impor-
tantly. "Let's see." He frowned
hard. "Where shall we look first?"

"I know," said Billy excitedly, "the
deserted house!" As soon as he'd
said it he wished he hadn't. He and

Pete hadn't been near the deserted house since the day they had discovered somebody living there, and Billy had no desire to go now.

"That might be a good idea," answered Pete slowly.

"Maybe not," Billy hurried to add. "Jimmy probably wouldn't have wandered that far away from home."

Pete looked at Billy with a half-smile on his face. "You scared?" he asked.

Billy flushed. "Of course not. I was just thinking that maybe we should go in the other direction, down by the river, or—" His voice trailed off.

"Yeah, maybe," agreed Pete.

Billy couldn't resist getting back at Pete. "You scared?" he asked.

"Me?" Pete acted surprised. "I'd go to that old deserted house any day or even at night. But I bet you wouldn't."

"I would too," Billy retorted. "I'll—I'll go right now."

"Okay, let's go then."

Frisky tagged along at Billy's heels not knowing the fear his master was feeling, the fear that whoever had his hideout in the old house would be there when they arrived.

16

At the Deserted House Again

Billy's heart began to pound wildly when the deserted house came into view through the trees. He glanced at Pete, who was carelessly hitting the underbrush with a big stick he had picked up along the way.

"I don't think Jimmy would go into the house," Billy said uneasily. "He's too little to climb in the window. Maybe if we searched the bushes around the house—"

"Yeah," agreed Pete. "We'll search the bushes."

They both fell silent as they neared the house. Billy had almost forgotten about finding Jimmy. He was only thinking about getting back to the safety of the road that led back to town.

As they came around the side of the house they saw the back door was half open. Frisky sniffed around excitedly, then dashed through the door into the house.

Billy gasped. "Pete, Frisky went in!" he said in a horrified whisper.

Pete nodded numbly, fear written on his face.

"I've got to go get him. Then let's get out of here."

Billy was glad that Pete followed him into the house. They tiptoed

through the kitchen and out into the hall just in time to see Frisky's white tail disappear at the top of the stairs.

Billy had never been so scared in his life, but he had to get Frisky. He couldn't leave his pup here with Old Man Hitchcock's ghost or whatever it was.

Frisky began to bark.

Billy and Pete took the steps two at a time. They had to stop him! They had to get him! The barking was coming from the occupied room. Billy stopped short at the open door. There on the floor sat Jimmy! His eyes were red from crying, but he was happy now with Frisky licking his face and jumping wildly about him.

"Jimmy!" gasped Billy. "What are you doing here? How did you find the deserted house?"

Then his eyes caught sight of the rope tied around Jimmy's waist and fastened to the iron bedstead. In an instant Billy understood. Jimmy hadn't come here by himself. Someone had brought him! The thought sent shivers up and down Billy's spine.

"Jimmy!" he cried, trying to undo the knotted rope around the boy's waist. "We've got to get out of here." His fingers felt like thumbs. Maybe

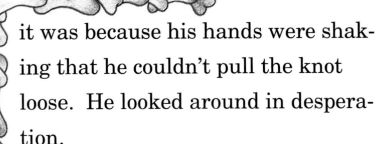

it was because his hands were shaking that he couldn't pull the knot loose. He looked around in desperation.

A sound at the door made them both twirl around. There stood an angry man. Billy gasped. It was the strange man he had seen in the park!

"What are you doing here in my house?" he demanded, taking a step toward Pete and closing his big hands around the boy's neck.

Frisky, always excited by a scuffle, jumped at the man's heels, barking loudly. When Frisky bit through his trousers, the man let go of Pete and turned on the dog.

Pete slipped out of the door. Billy couldn't escape, because the man was between him and the door. Besides, how could he leave Frisky and Jimmy? Billy's thoughts were all muddled. Then what he saw made him cry out in horror. The man was kicking Frisky with his heavy shoes.

Billy covered his eyes. With one last kick the man sent Frisky flying out of the room and slammed the door shut. Then he turned on Billy.

"What are you trying to do?" he demanded. "Steal my boy?"

Billy's mouth was so dry from fright he couldn't have answered even if he'd known what to say.

"At last I found my boy, and nobody's going to take him away from me this time," muttered the man. "Now all I have to do is find my wife, and I'll have my family again."

17

Prisoners!

Billy wanted to run, to scream, to do something, but he was too frightened. His legs felt like noodles. He stared at the man in terror. Jimmy started to whimper, "I want Mommy."

The man stooped down by the small boy and awkwardly stroked his hair. "Don't cry, son. I'll find your mommy. Then we'll all be happy again."

Suddenly Billy remembered the headline in the newspaper. Could this be the man who had escaped from the mental hospital? If only he

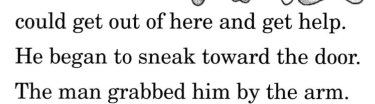

could get out of here and get help. He began to sneak toward the door. The man grabbed him by the arm.

"Not so fast, young man. You're not leaving. You might give away my secret. I'll find another length of rope for you."

Billy's heart pounded wildly as the man tied him securely with the rope. "Please, God," he said over and over in his heart, but he was too frightened to pray anything else.

"We know that all things work together for good to them that love God." The words flashed into his mind. Maybe the verse was true before, but not this time, he mused. Being captured by a crazy man couldn't be good for anything. Could it?

But all the other bad things had worked out for good, even Frisky's getting lost. Suddenly Billy remembered Frisky. Where was he? Was he lying under some bush dying all alone? And what about Jimmy? What would the crazy man do to them? Where was Pete?

The words came back to Billy: "*All things work together for good to them that love God.*" That meant everything! Gradually Billy's heart stopped beating so wildly. Jesus was with him even out here in the deserted house. He was with Jimmy, too, and Pete, and even Frisky.

The minutes dragged on. The strange man opened a can of beans and hungrily devoured them. Billy suddenly realized he was hungry. He had forgotten to make himself a sandwich as Aunt Kate had suggested. He glanced at Jimmy. The small boy, exhausted from crying, had curled up on the floor and fallen asleep.

Billy strained his ears for some sound that would tell him Frisky was still around. He could hear no familiar dog noises, just the singing of the birds and the buzzing of the insects of the woods.

The man walked back and forth nervously, in and out of the room. Then he lit a cigarette and sat down on the bed to smoke.

The minutes seemed like hours to Billy as he waited, listened, and

hoped. Suddenly he heard something. What was it? Voices? Somebody coming through the bushes? Somebody downstairs? The man heard it, too. He sprang up and looked around wildly.

At that moment the door burst open, and a police officer appeared.

"Well, here's our man!" he exclaimed to the other members of the search party who were right behind him. In a moment they had surrounded the escapee and put handcuffs on him. Realizing he was outnumbered, the mental patient did not resist.

"And here's Jimmy!" cried Mr. Parker, running to his son. The officer slashed the ropes that were tying

Billy and Jimmy. Mr. Parker picked up his son. Everybody talked at once. Pete stood in the background grinning.

As the officers were taking the strange man away, Mr. Parker turned to Billy and Pete. "I don't know how to thank you boys for finding Jimmy."

"It really wasn't us," answered Pete. "It was Frisky. We were just planning to look in the bushes, but Frisky ran into the house, so we came in, too. That's how we found Jimmy."

Mr. Parker said something about Frisky being the most wonderful dog in the world and deserving of a steak, but Billy hardly heard him.

Where was Frisky, anyway?

After the others had left, Billy and Pete searched the bushes around the deserted house for Frisky.

"Maybe he crawled away to die," said Pete, not knowing how sad his words made Billy feel. "Dogs do that when they get hurt bad."

Billy didn't answer. He couldn't. The lump in his throat was too big.

Then they found him, down by the creek behind the house. He had crawled under the bushes and was lying with his head on his paws, his eyes closed. Tenderly Billy picked him up and carried him home.

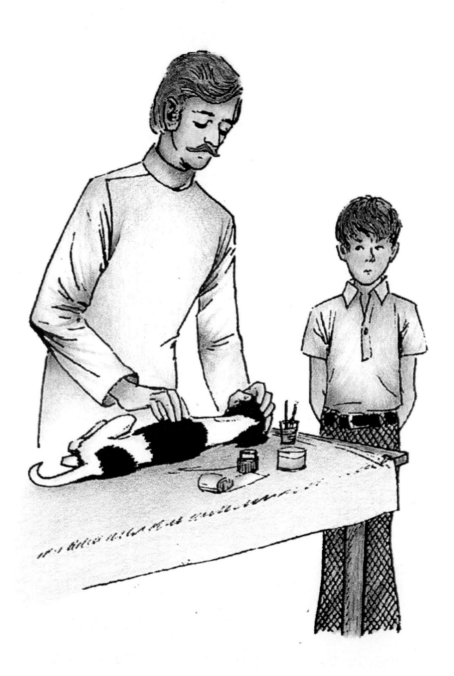

18
Part of God's Plan

"Your dog has been badly hurt," said the veterinarian as he examined Frisky. "I'm sorry, but there's nothing more I can do for him. Take him home and make him as comfortable as you can."

Aunt Kate said Frisky could sleep in Billy's room that night and Pete could stay overnight with Billy if his parents didn't mind.

Pete slept in Billy's bed, and Billy slept on the floor in a sleeping bag beside Frisky. Mrs. Parker had sent

over a steak for Frisky, but he was too sick to care about food. He didn't even want a drink of the warm milk that Aunt Kate had put in a dish for him.

Aunt Kate came and turned out the light. "Try to sleep now, boys," she said gently. "There's nothing more you can do for Frisky."

But Billy couldn't sleep. All he could do was think about Frisky.

"Billy," whispered Pete after a while. "You asleep?"

"No," Billy answered.

"Neither am I. I've been thinking about that guy grabbing me around the neck. Man, was that scary!"

"Yeah, I know. I was scared just watching."

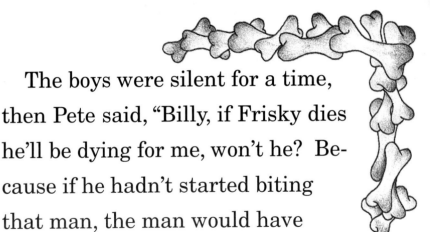

The boys were silent for a time, then Pete said, "Billy, if Frisky dies he'll be dying for me, won't he? Because if he hadn't started biting that man, the man would have killed me, maybe. But I got away, and the man hurt Frisky instead."

"Yeah, you're right," said Billy. When Pete talked about Frisky's dying, Billy hurt inside, but Pete's words made him think of something he'd been wanting Pete to understand. Billy raised up on one elbow.

"It's something like what Jesus did for you and me and everybody, Pete. On the cross. Remember that little picture I drew for you once?"

"Yeah, I remember."

"Jesus died in our place so we can live forever in heaven with God. He died for us, so we can go free."

Pete didn't answer. Billy dropped back on his pillow and stared into the darkness. "Please, God," he prayed silently, "help Pete to believe in You."

Billy thought Pete had fallen asleep until Pete called him again. "Hey, Billy."

"Yeah?"

"I've been thinking. Maybe I should start going to Sunday school with you. You still want me to?"

"Sure. Next Sunday, okay?"

"Okay."

Pete's words made Billy forget about the hurt inside him for a little

while. Could Frisky's getting hurt be part of God's plan to get Pete started going to Sunday school and believing on Him? A sense of awe filled Billy's heart. Wasn't God smart to be able to make *all things,* even the bad ones, work together for something good?

"He'll do what's best for Frisky," he told himself, suddenly feeling so drowsy he couldn't keep his eyes open.

Billy didn't know how long he'd been sleeping, but suddenly he was awake. For a moment he didn't re-member why he was lying on the floor in a sleeping bag instead of his bed. Slowly the events of the day before came back to him—going to

the deserted house, finding Jimmy,
Frisky getting hurt. He sat up. The
moon was shining into the room.
What was that noise?

Billy's heart gave a leap. It was
Frisky lapping up milk from the
dish. He was eating! He was better!

Billy jumped up and knelt on the
floor beside his pet. He stroked him
gently. Frisky wagged his tail fee-
bly and licked Billy's hand. A great
happiness stole into Billy's heart.
He knew Frisky was going to get
well!

19

The Big Secret

What was the secret Dad was talking about? Billy couldn't imagine. It must be something nice, because both Dad and Aunt Kate seemed so excited about it. Tonight they were all three going out to The Steakhouse for dinner, and Dad promised to tell the secret then.

When they got to the restaurant Dad said Billy could order anything he wanted, so Billy ordered a hamburger, french fries, and a chocolate milkshake. He hoped Aunt Kate wouldn't be able to finish her steak so he could take what was left home

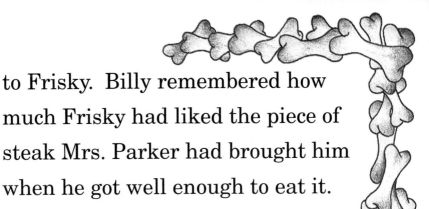

to Frisky. Billy remembered how
much Frisky had liked the piece of
steak Mrs. Parker had brought him
when he got well enough to eat it.

Mrs. Parker liked Frisky now.
She treated both Billy and Frisky
like heroes since they had found
Jimmy.

But what could Dad's secret be?

Dad waited until they were eating their dessert before he broke the
news. For a few minutes he simply
twitched his nose, twirled the end of
his mustache, and smiled. Then he
put his big hand over Billy's smaller
one.

"Billy," he said, "your Aunt Kate
and I have decided to get married."

177

Billy dropped his straw and stared at the couple across the table from him. Married! Then Aunt Kate would be his new mother! A slow grin spread over his face. "Hey, neat!" he said.

As soon as they came back from the restaurant Billy ran across the yard to tell Uncle John the wonderful news.

"And then they talked about a honeymoon," said Billy. "What is a honeymoon like, Uncle John?"

The older man's eyes twinkled. "I reckon a boy your age and a bachelor my age wouldn't understand much about honeymoons." He shrugged his shoulders. "It's really

just a trip, Billy, taken by a newly married couple."

"And us," put in Billy. "Pete and you and me. They said we could come along and camp. Aunt Kate isn't used to tents, so they'll stay in the hotel nights, but they'll be with us sometimes during the day. Oh boy, will we have fun!"

"I told you there was a camping trip in the offing," Uncle John reminded him with a chuckle. "What about Frisky? I suppose the Parkers would be willing to keep him for you."

"I'll go ask Aunt Kate," answered Billy, turning to run across the yard to his own house. He was back in a moment with a big smile on his face.

"You'd never guess what Aunt Kate said, Uncle John."

"Then you had better tell me."

"Aunt Kate said, 'Frisky is going along, of course. We can't leave part of the family behind!'"

Uncle John laughed. "Now, what do you know about that!" he exclaimed. Uncle John kept on talking, but Billy didn't hear him. He was busy saying thank you to God for working everything out for good as He had promised. Yes, God was able to use all things in His plans—even Frisky!